I0715720

Thought Here
Would Cure Me of There

María Luisa Arroyo Cruzado

LILY POETRY REVIEW BOOKS

Table of Contents

to stop my body & mind from withdrawing
from known joys

after New England trees shuddered & shed
their last leaves

I thought I had to flee, to cross this country
to desert & days

with piercing blue & burning & walls

thought here
would cure me of there

I needed to escape the mummified mice
in walls, under electric oven, beneath the asthmatic
fridge, the heavy squirrels
bounding in the attic
a romper room for their newborn
the sagging front porch
too hot to read in, the sun magnified
through windows that killed
the wasps & bees & spiders
seeking shade, a brother's pressure
to buy a dying house
with my aging mother
still in it

perhaps I imagined this:
a man as a human life raft
for this life I flung
across 2500 miles

the blurring of cities & bridges
through days of driving
& nights with one eye open
in hotel rooms that reek
of antiseptic dreams

how I disregarded the beauty
of that marvelous journey
by myself, thinking then
that it mattered less

because I was alone

because it was
only me

one month after Mother's Day
the news of my move
cross country to no family
into the arms of a man
no one met
blew my family sideways
like these bending palm trees
in this Nevada dust storm
winds galloping
from the desert
stampeding down grids
of streets, their howls scraping
tall walls
insulating isolating
me

I fell in love with his childhood memories:
his Mississippi Grandma
scrubbing him in a shiny metal tub
white washcloth wrapped
around white soap

his Mississippi Grandpa
sending him, just two,
to pee in the outhouse
like a man

how she swept smooth
the esses that snakes make
on the dirt floor
of their shack

how he howled when Grandpa beat
all the grandkids
for the transgressions
of one

perhaps I used this man
brown & native & bald
Mississippi born
Pasadena raised
kissable lips, hands addicted
to squeezing my generous breasts & nipples
naked & through my shirt
in bed & before work & in the car
his body aroused behind me in bed
his melting sighs
at the Spanish of his name
rolling in my mouth
my tongue on his body
how he'd touch & pull the s-curls
of my black & white hair
amazed
at its instant memory

to see him walking nude
fluid mahogany
his belly round with beer

to become spellbound by a Mississippi man
broken like this:

inhaling cannabis
more deeply than air
before & after work

driving to Primm
every second Saturday
to place bets with money
meant for rent

slipping a cheap ashtray
into the wide mouth of my purse
under casino lights & cameras

perhaps you used me like I used you
the soft mattress of the queen bed I bought
an island we shared
to keep each other alive
in sleep

your strangled breaths
after long moments in your chest
years of brain cells deprived of air
poking holes in your memory
of how to do things awake

my survival
depending on sleep
on my right side
my throat safe
from the constricting
gurgle & heave
of achalasia

I had to lie
to make him pack & move out, said
he couldn't live with me anymore
my mother was flying to Vegas
& there couldn't be
any signs of *his* life
in *my* home

before my lie
it wasn't enough for him
that I
no longer wanted his habit
of forgetting to hide
his addictions

in my lie, he understood "mother"
losing his three years ago
losing his last photos of her in the hospital
when he updated his phone
writing & circling her birthday on the calendar,
10 days before mine, telling me
after packing his last tote
to tell my mother
he said hi
forgetting
she erased him
from my life
almost as fast
as I did

the red cliffs are not moved by my misery
neither are the tourists with sensible shoes
for rocky paths, floppy hats
against the pulsing sun
socks high on ankles against sudden slithers
who ignore me alone
in pajamas & sandals, my bedhead hair
on this burning bench, waiting
for him
to finally
move out

what in me
needs to deny myself
freedom
again?

this time, I chose the promise of love
with a man with champagne dreams
of a million-dollar home in DelMar, exotic
fish in a home aquarium, greenhouse
leafy with cannabis
a private pool
by the ocean
he'll never swim in

to burst the apartment silence
after my breakup
I look for stamps & human contact
at a post office

the Google Maps app leads me to a dingy spot

pot fumes punch the path to the glass door
"No sales. Only pickups…"

I leave & arrive
at some dusty plaza
paper scraps skipping & sailing

a saint
painted on the wall
between a dollar store with grimy windows
& Cardenas Supermarket
is smiling, his hands
cupping a wooden bowl
for me

San Pascual Bailón smiles from his shack
above his friar haircut
chili peppers, red votive candles, hang by his pans
a short white one burns ten points of light
behind his brown robed shoulder

I want his bliss, to touch
his painted smile behind the blue mailbox bolted
to the concrete sidewalk, count
the Monarch butterflies painted
huge to small, all born to fly
in a rabble, a kaleidoscope
of wings at summer's end
flapping north for eight weeks
to die & become reborn

in week 4 at the One Stop I resign
delete the Google number
assigned to receive the daily deluge
of strangers seeking trainings & dollars
this subcontractor mismanages

no longer will my voice sweet
with hope ask my script
of transactional intrusions

on this side of the number
systems freeze grants lock caseloads
unassigned reassigned up in the air who left now
languish

supervisors squawk:
the numbers! the numbers!

orientations I give
virtually on Wednesdays
about state funding for x & y?

lost reallocated rules changed
by Fridays

I will
not
turn 55
like this

open-hearted woman from Mississippi, neighbor
here in concrete honeycombs
in the desert for seniors
I bring you roses, my thanks
for safeguarding deliveries
to my doorstep
during my winter days
on the East Coast

you invite me in
to wildly blooming aloe, blessings
painted on white walls & your worried spirit

you point to some broken
leaves, show me spilled
detergent, piles of empty
hangers, dirty handprints
around doorjambs & near knobs, all
while you were sleeping.

you too
have been hurt
by a man

at Menchi's Frozen Yogurt, I watch you
purple hoodie hiding your face

you daintily press
with your slim brown hand
tiny dollops of frozen sweetness
into sample cups you slurp

I say my name, tell you I teach
& offer to pay for a cup
as large as mine

as you walk beside me
pulling levers & sprinkling crushed candy
you tell me how this manager
lets you come every day after school
for free samples, her own kids' heads
bowed over homework,
how scared you feel
about 9th grade,
how …

this desert highway leads me past
exits for the Grand Canyon
the last gas station for miles
short wire fences to keep
cattle & government secrets
to hills of roads sloping up
5300 feet
to an Arizona view
of Thumb Butte
Granite Mountain
the sun rising
at 6:39
her rays called & interwoven
for generations
by women
Yavapai
into baskets
here in Prescott
my first dawn
at 55

Mami misses me, reminisces
about our 12 days in Puerto Rico
as she carefully flips the pages
of our photo books printed
in the January of our return

Mami misses me & yet her "¡no!"
on our Saturday coast to coast call
doesn't leave any room
for the briefly hopeful "oo"
in my American "no?"

she misses me but not flying
she wants me there
to drink Bustelo coffee brewed
with a cloth filter, to eat
her "ssshhhh", hot grilled cheese
sizzling with butter, to play
hours of Yahtzee, our cackling
ricocheting
around the rooms
of her new home, a condo nestled
atop a manmade hill
across the steep street
from a monastery

she wants me to touch
her money tree, see
the five-trunked birch
by her front door, feel
the warm air steaming up vents
even in the bathroom, smell
the candles she burns
in the spacious living room, pray
at the ones at her altar
of santos & santas
as sacred to her
as my family of books

the post office employee denied
my request for a RealID
the December of my trip with Mami
to Puerto Rico, the archipelago
where the stems of our umbilical cords
are buried with bendiciones

for 54 years
the U.S. government erased
Cruzado
my mother
from my last name

ruled
Arroyo
my father's
last name
enough

the blank spaces in Mami's short-term memory are growing

is that why she doesn't trust herself
white-haired woman now 78
to walk alone cane in hand
down the steep hill to Riverdale Road
to discover where to play her numbers?

or to cross the street to pray
alongside monks & nuns?

or perhaps she anticipates the dangers all the time & not only
during the ten days of my winter visit:
the 25-year-old woman & her dog
walking the same path & time every sunset
are killed by a car on the road
Mami would have walked

on Riverdale Road
lightning knocked down live wires
hissing across four lanes
blue lights orbing
for hours

at 78, Mami still trusts me
her only daughter to hold
her factory-hardened hands, clip
her thick curving toenails, massage
the dry flaking skin of her sturdy legs, rub
the tops & soles of her broad brown feet, lay
hands at the nape of her neck, lie
a guestroom away, listening
to her sleeping breaths

eight months in
I still don't understand
the terms of survival here:
pawn shops for cars & pay
alerts against monsoons & dust storms
the summer melt of tires spinning at 70 mph
throngs without homes, sleeping
on sidewalks, under the shaded arc
of bridges, by the wrought iron gates
of cemeteries, under blue tarps
behind fast food dumpsters

the closer to downtown I drive
the more frenzied the taps
at stoplights

but I won't return
to where the roots of my spirit started to rot
in a workplace that muzzled my voice
in a two-family home overrun
with mice & a second mortgage
swallowing money
for a handicapped accessible bathroom
my father, double amputee & blind,
never used
before he died
my mother
bathing him
for ten years
like an ailing brother
in their bed

did I inherit my father's fathomless ache
to be loved?

the source of his hunger, mother dying in birth
his two-year-old self, inconsolable
his grandmother's grip on his life
that never stopped draining
like blood into earth
like ten years later, his father collapsing
in the cane field, machete wound still splitting
his skull under straw hat, never fully healing
his grandmother again
gripping his life
stunned

I fall too easily
for the music
of a man's voice
when he wants me
when he wants
to learn how to reshape
his mouth & tongue
to utter the accent
over my i:
María

your Black Virginia drawl
sang my name
seven years ago

we talked about Baldwin's essays
as you drove your eighteen-wheeler
up & down
our East Coast, answered
my worries
about your locomotion
in places dangerous
for you, made plans
to make love
somewhere
in between
our voices

that season of dying aunts & Mami's severe
lightning storms in her face, I prayed
to the Universe to take
a year off my life
to give to Mami

yes
your romantic loving was cold
my widowed Beloved
your first marriage arranged
by Nigerian fathers
but your passions for fasting
to become closer to God
your 5 a.m. prayer circles by phone
your swaying back to me in bed
you then kneeling naked
at my feet
urging me to pray
for healing not the loss
of any day of my life
tethered me
to you

I might have to give up on men

the Baldwin-listening truck driver
the passionately fasting, cold-loving pastor
the charismatic PCA with champagne dreams
the IT specialist dancing naked in his video

they
mistook me
my lusciously fat, honey-hued body
as a submissive female form

they ignored the clarity
of my words & wants

already predetermined the way
to perceive & receive me

as if

being confident & intelligent & so certain
about all that I want
in this female body
so lusciously fat & honey-hued
are lies

once I tried to date a White man

in the Barnes & Noble café, J. rambled
about how I was among many
women of this age
looking for a man like him, widowed,
to like & perhaps love

when a friend of mine, waving, stopped by,
J., still a stranger, rambled
to her
about how I was among many
women of this age
looking for a man like him, widowed,
to like & perhaps love

I leapt into the voice of another new man for lust
trusted him only with my words
in texts & phone calls
not with my body

I wanted to feel
control & desire

he wanted
to be controlled by my words

the more he told me
how he wanted
to be controlled

the more I lost myself
again

how was I supposed to know
that the summer of 2004 would be my last
with a lover who'd whisper mi gordita en el cielo
my grad school apartment 21 stories up
by the Charles River

he'd answer my calls
for daytime loving, trace
the features of my face
give & receive besos
(no rush) undress
himself & me, lead me to my bed
(no rush), stroke my skin,
pero qué maravillosa tú eres
guiding my hands down his body
as if work
didn't need our attention

my nostalgia now
is not about mourning him
it's about mourning
how the few men
I've loved ever since
never loved
themselves enough
to consume me

I don't know
how to say "mental illness"
in the Spanish of my family

Abuela's failed cure for bedwetting:
pee on a brick she heated
in the oven, its steam rising up
to exorcise el problema
plaguing me allá 'bajo

whenever she saw me reading,
odious fear crawled up in her,
made her spit: ¡Loca!

the same disease, she hisses,
of reading too much lived in her son,
Tío Beto, the one in Puerto Rico

who tried to crush the life & spells
out of her, a malevolent unknown,
sang the murmuring voices, not
the woman who birthed & raised him

Abuela, which spells failed you then?

I still don't know
how to say "mental illness"
in our Spanish

even in the desert I have to fight
my brain's winter chemistry

how it breaks
my body's rhythm for sleep, beats
my thoughts into frenzy, burns
holes in nascent poems
turns
them & me
into ash

when the panic attack crushed
my chest, knocked
my heart into palpitations, I gave up
my fast from paraxotine
sought an online doctor for a script
received it rushed, uncapped
the green bottle of pills, oblong & scored
710 on one side, HH
on the other because journaling
in sunny Nevada
for my brain's chemistry
was not
enough

I read of augers & bores & saws
to drill & cut small sections in the living skull

of leeches latching & opening veins
to balance the humors in body & mind

of rest cures & isolation
some for a season
others, a lifetime

of ice water baths & restraints
insulin comas & shock therapy

of cut connections in five minutes
between prefontal & frontal lobes

for men, for children, for women like me
to alleviate headaches & demons

doubt divides me
in the oval floor-length mirror

one arm ringed gangrene black & red
the other raised, a brown elephant's trunk
amputated from my body

where did my writing hand go?

my breasts, green globes
float

no torso
only a sagging
pendulum of a body
striped black

I seek my face
see only empty red sockets

the half moon of my face
in shadow

my neck
a brown triangle
balancing my bald head

is this how my son
twelve years old then
saw me
when he painted
this?

it's too late to learn my family history
of mental illnesses, many buried
under addictions
many misnamed
as demonios

the questions I carry
will remain
unfurled maps

whenever I felt threatened
en el español de mi papá
I rushed into the safety
of my teachers' American English

the Romans & Greeks greeted us
in Mr. Dennis' classes, their words
new codes & symbols for the notes
Tee & I wrote
about high school crushes

fiery Frau Professorin Margrit Lichterfeld
challenged me to rewrite
deutsche Märchen & stories
mit stärken HeldInnen

I don't remember the name
of my Russian instructor
just the soap opera, "Da dzvidania, li-ehta"
stick figures with emojis

when German became meine Liebessprache
with the confident Iranian dancing
among the Greeks, Farsi:
zaban-e ou, zaban-e Hafez, zaban-e Rumi
bonded me to him & his parents

every language I learn
becomes a secret room in my head

and yet the language of depression
eludes me, my amygdala
swelling, my hippocampus
shriveling, those systems
misfiring

it helps me to know that depression
is "more complex
than brain chemical imbalance"

I used to think
that if I forced myself
to trigger happy chemical reactions:
write down every day in my journal
three things that'll bring me joy
think positive thoughts
surround myself with hues of light & sky
play music
smile smile smile
& smile some more
en mal tiempo, buena cara
give away my time because others deserve it
more than I do & it'll make me feel
worthy

in this desert daylight
with no shadows & no shade
they are placebo effects

in this desert daylight
with no shadows & no shade
I am now growing
like the stubborn pine trees
transplanted trunks buried & hand watered
to thrive
shedding old needles
to make room

perhaps a part of me sought this desert city
as a possible place
for me to abandon a self
in the barren red cliffs, unrelenting
heat, rocks underfoot sharp
& burning, no water, brittle
brush, no sounds of crawling
life, diamond yellow sign to warn
parked travelers
to check under vehicles
for tortoises
seeking relief

how I miss my family of books, more
than 100 numbered boxes
in Springfield storage

every time I join a reading online, I scan
the squares for lit screens, yearn
for the scent only books
catch & release
in the homes of readers

here
is not home
but Binghamton will be

soon
I will pack my life
& the same five boxes of books
I brought with me
three seasons ago
into my Honda, donate
the rest, drive
cross country again
arrive this time
to a life
capacious enough
to bring my family
home

when I move from desert to four seasons
I will leave the saguaro skeleton
of myself behind, admire
her & her journey
from the distance
of my new emergence
in the four living languages
of my self-forgiving spirit

the heart you mailed arrived today
black & gray rock
rough with flecks of light

how did you know
that I need to hold
myself?

see how the broad flat leaves of this cactus spread
like the wings of green angels & swans

reach to stroke the leaf's skin
between the turgid thorns & weeping brown scars

desire to touch the lush round red
of prickly pears, these nopales
sprouting & ripening around its edges

this is how my freedom now feels

Acknowledgments

Grateful acknowledgment is made
to the following magazine,
in which these poems will appear:

Lily Poetry Review: "[to stop my body & mind from withdrawing]",
"[perhaps I imagined this]", "[I don't know]"

Born in Manati, Puerto Rico, & raised in Springfield, MA, María Luisa Arroyo Cruzado earned a BA (Colby) & MA in German (Tufts), her third language; & an MFA from the Solstice MFA Program. María Luisa writes poetry & creative nonfiction prose that code-switch between English, Spanish, German, & Farsi—the cultural languages of her experiences.

María Luisa's poetry collections include *Landscapes: photos & poems* (2023), *Destierro Means More than Exile* (2018); & *Gathering Words: Recogiendo palabras* (2008). *Resistencia: Resilience* (2023) is her first collection that contains both poetry & creative nonfiction essays. In March 2024, she edited & published her first anthology, *Pán•o•ply,* through her literary imprint, MultiCreative Wisdom, which focuses on creative writing by individuals who self-identify as BIPOC & female or non-binary.

In recognition for her literary citizenship as a poet & intersectional feminist educator, María Luisa was named a 2008 Massachusetts Unsung Heroine & the inaugural poet laureate of Springfield, MA (2014-2016). María Luisa was also awarded a 2014 Carlos Vegas Social Justice Award & a 2018 NEPR Arts &Humanities Award. Receiving an honorary doctorate from Smith College in May 2024 continues to recognize María Luisa for her two intersecting practices.

As a Clark Diversity Fellow, María Luisa is joyfully pursuing her PhD in Comparative Literature at Binghamton University.